SOUTH OAKLAND COUNTY

OPPOSITE: The legendary flyover bridge elevates Woodward Avenue over Eight Mile Road, the boundary between Detroit and Wayne County to the south and Oakland County to the north. Routed as M-102 for most of its length, Eight Mile has, since the 1950s, come to represent a psychological, racial, and physical dividing line between city and suburb. In recent years, however, racial integration in South Oakland County has diminished the thoroughfare's stigma.

THEN & NOW

SOUTH OAKLAND COUNTY

Paul Vachon

To Sheryl, my wife of 25 years and to our son, Evan, who everyday makes me proud to be a father.

ISBN 978-0-7385-8311-2

Library of Congress Control Number: 2011927875

Published by Arcadia Publishing
Charleston, South Carolina

Printed in the United States of America

For all general information, please contact Arcadia Publishing:
Telephone 843-853-2070
Fax 843-853-0044
E-mail sales@arcadiapublishing.com
For customer service and orders:
Toll-Free 1-888-313-2665

Visit us on the Internet at www.arcadiapublishing.com

On the Front Cover: Decades of prosperity provided by the automotive industry have blessed Oakland County with a legendary affluence. Few places offer greater evidence of this than Birmingham, which is home to professionals from the "Detroit Three" (Ford, General Motors, and Chrysler) and numerous other fields. Along with neighborhoods such as Bloomfield Hills, Troy, Huntington Woods, and West Bloomfield Township, Birmingham is largely responsible for making Oakland the fourth-wealthiest county in the United States, among those with a population exceeding one million. (Historical image courtesy Walter Reuther Library, Wayne State University.)

On the Back Cover: Surrounded by Royal Oak and Ferndale, tiny Pleasant Ridge, with a population of 2,500, ranks as the smallest incorporated city in Michigan. Subdivided from the Mayday Farm by Burt Taylor in 1913, the community was officially established as a village in 1921 and as a city in 1927. Proud of its independence and its diminutive size, Pleasant Ridge recently remade its miniature police shack into its historical museum. (Courtesy Walter Reuther Library, Wayne State University.)

CONTENTS

ACKNOWLEDGMENTS

As I neared completion of this book, I was reminded of the second corollary of the famed Murphy's Law, "Everything will take longer than you think it will." Writing Then & Now: *South Oakland County* was certainly no exception. Obtaining vintage images from over 20 different sources, taking the counterpart photographs, and doing the background research along with other related tasks tested my patience.

Special thanks go to my editor, Anna Wilson. Despite having to deal with several different authors and constantly struggling to meet deadlines, her help was always just a phone call or e-mail away.

I want to thank the many kind and helpful people without whose help this book would not have been possible: Garry Andrews, Ferndale Historical Museum; Nancy Beets, Southfield Public Library; Jeffery Brieger, Oakland Pioneer Historical Society; Scott Burnstein; Judith Cantor, Congregation Shaarey Zedek archives; George Cartsonis, Oakland Community College; Marcin Chumiecki, Orchard Lake Schools; Janet Durecki, Rabbi Leo M. Franklin Archives at Temple Beth El; Thomas Featherstone and Elizabeth Clemens, Walter Reuther Library for Urban and Labor Affairs, Wayne State University; Roberta Frey Gilboe, Cranbrook Academy of Art; Jack Houlihan, Shrine of the Little Flower; Shelly Kemp, Royal Oak Chamber of Commerce; William Lamott, Franklin Historical Society; Pam Lightbody, Northland Center; Robert Machus; Michael McPhee, Oakland County Boat Club; Robert Morosi, Michigan Department of Transportation; Melody Nichols, Clawson Historical Society; Robert Ortlieb, William Beaumont Hospital; Robert Osborne, Somerset Collection; Shirley Pauquette, Oakland University; James Petrocela, Rochester Hills Community Library; Edmund Richardson, Pontiac Public Library; Carol Ring, Berkley Historical Society; Keith Brown and Robin Roberts, Lathrup Village Historical Society; Ruth Stiegel, Farmington Community Library; Robert Tansey Jr., Somerset Buick GMS; Darla Van Hoey, Southfield Historical Society; and Jayne Zellers, Kirk in the Hills.

My thanks also go to my wife, Sheryl, for her proofreading expertise and to fellow author Maureen McDonald for being a "second pair of eyes" by reviewing the manuscript.

Unless otherwise noted, all contemporary images are courtesy of the author.

Introduction

Oakland County, with its contrasting ethnic groups, cultures, and income levels, in many ways represents a microcosm of the Midwestern United States. Part urban, part suburban, and in many places part rural, Oakland's diversity and division, as well as its successes and failures, have largely typified the character of postwar suburbia that was repeated throughout the nation with only slight variations.

This is not to say, however, that Oakland lacks its own individual character. The county's persona is in many ways an extension of the city of Detroit: hard working, religious, and economically centered on the auto industry but shifting gradually towards diversification. This is only half of the story though. Having experienced phenomenal growth since the 1960s, Oakland developed a unique side as well. As the auto industry matured during the postwar years, the county became home to many of its senior managers and executives. This affluence produced storied houses of worship, prestigious educational institutions, well-to-do residential neighborhoods, and upscale shopping and dining venues. Over time, Oakland became less a bedroom satellite of Detroit and more an autonomous community.

Despite this, Oakland's leaders are very much aware of the economic and political roles the county plays in greater Detroit and in all of Michigan. Realizing that 21st-century problems of infrastructure, transportation, and homeland security demand regional approaches, citizens of Michigan's second-largest county now appropriately see their community as part of "Metro Detroit."

The historical background behind Oakland's ascent is equally interesting. Prior to 1800, several Indian tribes inhabited virtually all of present-day lower Michigan. The dominant tribes were the Chippewa (Ojibwa), the Potawatomi, and the Ottawa, all of who spoke a dialect of Algonquin, the language of their common ancestral tribe of the same name. Throughout the 19th century, the Native American presence gradually diminished due to disease, removal laws enacted by hostile white authorities, and by cultural assimilation.

Oakland County was officially established on January 12, 1819, by Michigan governor Lewis Cass. Entrepreneurs from Detroit and elsewhere formed the Pontiac Company, which was dedicated to building the area's infrastructure. The city of Pontiac was established as the county seat largely for strategic reasons, as its central location minimized travel times. As Oakland gradually developed into an agricultural area during the 19th century, most towns—especially Pontiac—sprouted necessary support facilities, such as gristmills, feed stores, implement merchants, and the like. Shipment of crops was made possible by newly developed roads that traced the routes of early Indian trails. Today, Woodward Avenue follows the path of the old Saginaw Trail, while Orchard Lake Road is built along the Shiawassee Trail. By the close of the 19th century, the burgeoning county was firmly developed as a thriving agricultural area.

By the 1890s, the southern tier of the county began to develop along more residential lines. The area now known as Royal Oak began as a community called Urbanrest. As nearby Detroit became more industrialized, many former farmers moved south to claim factory jobs. At the same time, wealthy Detroit residents began to settle in various South Oakland locales, which would later become the neighborhoods of Birmingham, Bloomfield Hills, and Huntington Woods.

Contemporary Oakland County has grown in tandem with all of southeast Michigan. It has accomplished much and continues to evolve, enjoying bright prospects for its future.

CHAPTER 1

Lower Woodward

Owing to its proximity to Detroit, the southeast corner of Oakland County, including the communities of Ferndale and Royal Oak, experienced the earliest development and today exudes a retro, quasi-urban feel. This image from the late 1950s depicts an idyllic scene along Nine Mile Road, when neighborhood shopping was in its heyday. Today, the strip is home to bars, used bookstores, vintage clothing shops, and Affirmations, a community center serving the gay and lesbian population. (Historical image courtesy Ferndale Historical Museum.)

The styles and makes of cars traveling Woodward Avenue are not the only changes along this famed street. Traditional businesses like insurance agencies, car dealers, and drugstores have given way to those that give Ferndale its current Bohemian atmosphere, such as coffeehouses, pubs, and music venues like the Magic Bag Theater. Note the physical improvements, including the elimination of the parking lot inside the median. (Historical image courtesy Ferndale Historical Museum.)

Towering above the intersection of Nine Mile Road and Woodward Avenue was the Ferndale location of Federal's Department Store, one of several locally owned large stores that flourished from the 1950s through the 1970s. Existing very much as a neighborhood institution, Federal's served a middle-class clientele to whom they sold moderately priced clothing, shoes, and home accessories. After ceasing operations, the old building was demolished, and the site was redeveloped. Until recently, the location was home to an Old Navy outlet. (Historical image courtesy Ferndale Historical Museum.)

In what must be one of the most novel methods of advertising anywhere, the gimmick used by Wetmore's has few equals. Ever since 1928, the full-serve auto repair shop has promoted its wheel-alignment service by placing an older car in the tower over the shop, where it continuously spins its front wheels in a wobbly fashion, thanks to an innovative belt-drive system. Time has proven the effectiveness of this concept, both in the 1950s and today. (Historical image courtesy Ferndale Historical Museum.)

The city of Ferndale takes great pride in honoring its heritage. This is evidenced by the return of the iconic crow's nest to the intersection of Woodward Avenue and Nine Mile Road. In 2005, the Ferndale Historical Commission chose sculptor Shan Sutherland, a graduate of the Cranbrook Academy of Art, to create a replica of the original, which had offered police a safe and effective vantage point from which to direct traffic. The structure was used until 1928, when the introduction of electric traffic lights made it obsolete. The contemporary version, completed as part of a median improvement project, thoughtfully honors the past. (Historical image courtesy Ferndale Historical Museum.)

Perhaps the most recognizable landmark in Ferndale is the Ferndale Center Building, located at Woodward Avenue and Nine Mile Road. Originally named the C.H. Harrison Building, it was built by Clifford H. Harrison, president of the Ferndale Board of Commerce, in 1929. Despite the name, Harrison's own businesses had little actual presence in the building. Constructed as a real estate investment, it was home to Ferndale's city office and courtrooms. After moving in 1937 to a former bank building, the community finally built its first dedicated city hall in 1965. (Historical image courtesy Ferndale Historical Museum.)

Construction of the Woodward Avenue flyover bridge prompted advertisers to take advantage of a captive audience. The enormous AC Sparkplug billboard served as a stunning example. In 1908, French émigré and motorcycle racer Albert Champion established the company bearing his initials after fellow investors dismissed him from his first company, Champion Ignition Company. In 1927, AC Sparkplugs was purchased by General Motors and added to its corporate empire. In today's more diversified economy, the space is used by the Detroit Medical Center. (Historical image courtesy Ferndale Historical Museum.)

Perhaps more than surrounding communities, Ferndale pays considerable honor to its war veterans. The monument to residents who served in the Korean conflict is one among several that were moved from their original locations (this one being in the Woodward Avenue median) to the grassy island along Livernois Avenue during the 1980s. The quieter new location is much more conducive to reflection. (Historical image courtesy Ferndale Historical Museum.)

Construction of the Shrine of the Little Flower Church on Woodward Avenue at Twelve Mile Road began in 1932, shortly after completion of the tower and narthex. The pastor, Rev. Charles Coughlin, financed the project with donations from his nationwide radio audience. Initiated in 1926, the broadcasts first focused solely on religious themes, but as the Depression worsened, Coughlin's speeches took on a politically right-wing and anti-Semitic tone, resulting eventually in his censure. Today, the church enjoys its status as one of metro Detroit's premier Catholic congregations. The contemporary view of the roof is quite dramatic, despite having to be photographed through a screen. (Historical image courtesy Shrine of the Little Flower.)

Shortly before the completion of the new church in 1936, the original shrine was destroyed by fire. The tragedy proved strangely coincidental; in 1925, shortly after opening, the Ku Klux Klan had burned a cross in front of the church. Reverend Coughlin chose to build the new edifice from limestone, the tower of which formed a "cross they could not burn." Today, the foundation of the original church encloses a beautiful prayer garden. (Historical image courtesy Walter Reuther Library, Wayne State University.)

The intersection of Main and Fourth Streets emerged during the early 20th century as the banking area of Royal Oak. During a 1996 restoration of the Main Professional Building (the dark brick building in the upper left-hand corner), a name was discovered on the exterior of the building confirming the location as the second home of the Royal Oak Savings Bank. In 1916, the institution moved across Fourth Street to a massive Corinthian-columned bank structure. In recognition of its historical significance, the building recently escaped demolition. (Historical image courtesy Walter Reuther Library, Wayne State University.)

After the Royal Oak Savings Bank closed in the wake of the 1931 bank holiday, the grand building at 400 South Main Street was home to the Wayne-Oakland Bank, a regional institution until it was absorbed in a series of bank mergers. Today, the building has found new life as Metals in Time, a fine jewelry store offering top-notch merchandise and service. (Historical image courtesy Royal Oak Chamber of Commerce.)

The Detroit Zoo, actually located in Royal Oak and Huntington Woods, ranks as one of the most innovative zoos in the nation. For decades, the original 1928 aviary displayed an array of exotic birds. In 2000, the building was completely renovated and now serves as the Wildlife Interpretive Gallery, offering wildlife education through multimedia exhibits. Attached wings include the Matilda Wilson Free Flight Aviary and the Butterfly and Hummingbird Garden, unique attractions among American zoos. (Historical image courtesy Walter Reuther Library, Wayne State University.)

Until well into the 1970s, large national retailers often dominated the downtowns of America. Their recognizable names offered familiarity to visitors but also sacrificed a town's local identity. Today, many of these behemoth stores have given way to a new class of creative entrepreneurs, and this change is demonstrated in these images. The old Kresge store on Washington Avenue in Royal Oak is now home to Lily's Seafood and Café Muse, which is flanked by The Fifth, a high-rise luxury condo tower. (Historical image courtesy Royal Oak Chamber of Commerce.)

By 1950, phenomenal growth in south Oakland County created the need for a new community hospital. In 1953, ground was broken on what was to be called Oakland Hospital, built off Thirteen Mile Road in Royal Oak. When a shipment of building supplies was inadvertently delivered to Oakwood Hospital in Dearborn, the need for a new name became apparent. The decision was made to name the hospital after William Beaumont, a surgeon in the US Army who had served at Fort Mackinac on Mackinac Island during the early 19th century. Almost 60 years of growth and near constant expansion have made Beaumont one of the finest facilities in the United States. (Historical image courtesy William Beaumont Hospital.)

Admission procedures have certainly changed at Beaumont since its 1955 opening. What began as a 238-bed hospital has grown to become a system of three regional facilities, anchored by the Royal Oak location. Over the years, Beaumont has been the site of numerous medical firsts, including a 2003 milestone when stem cells from a patient's own blood were used to repair cardiac damage caused by a heart attack. The hospital recently received approval to develop a liver transplant program. (Historical image courtesy William Beaumont Hospital.)

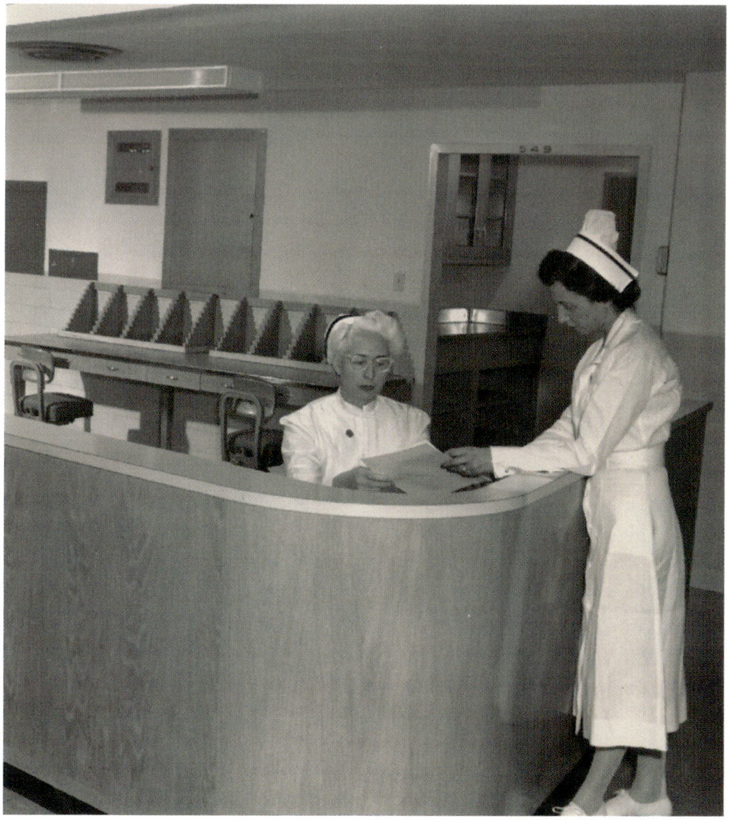

Acquiring state-of-the-art medical technology has contributed to Beaumont's success, involving all phases of patient care. The stunning contrast in the sophistication of a typical nurse's station illustrates this evolution. In 2007, Beaumont took delivery of a 128-slice Siemens cardiac CT scanner, one of only four such machines in the country. (Historical image courtesy William Beaumont Hospital.)

Since 1906, Roseland Park Cemetery has served as a place of tranquil beauty for the deceased. The original gate and mausoleum, designed by legendary Detroit architect Louis Kamper, blend with the newer structures, including the Resurrection Chapel, which features a reproduction of Da Vinci's *The Last Supper*. (Historical image courtesy Berkley Historical Society.)

The small city of Berkley, shoehorned between Royal Oak and Southfield, represents south Oakland's version of small-town America. What was once just an interurban stop between Detroit and Pontiac, the city has evolved into a mature, middle-class community that continually works to grow and renew itself. By the 1970s, what had been the rustic corner of Woodward Avenue and Twelve Mile Road became home to Berkley Plaza, a facility with retail stores and professional services. (Historical image courtesy Berkley Historical Society.)

By 1921, the number of Roman Catholics in Berkley became large enough to warrant the construction of a church. A small structure was built at Robina Street and Catalpa Avenue and served as a mission of St. Mary's parish in Royal Oak. Once designated a parish, the name was changed to Our Lady of Refuge, and the church was moved to its current location at Coolidge Highway and Harvard Street. In 1934, the name was changed to Our Lady of La Salette. In later years, Anderson Middle School was built on the original site. (Historical image courtesy Berkley Historical Society.)

The community of Clawson, a small suburb flanked by Royal Oak and Troy, still manages to present an idyllic small-town feel despite many modern changes. The Clawson Theater was built in 1940 and featured a stripped-down art moderne facade. The theater closed in the early 1960s, and the building has been adapted to accommodate the Gourmet Coffee Shop. Sharing the block is the Ambassador Roller Rink, a longtime fixture that closed recently. That building is now home to Leon & Lulu, an offbeat furniture and novelty store. (Historical image courtesy Clawson Historical Society.)

One of the most enduring trends in American business is the gradual yet constant shift towards greater specialization within all industries. At one time, the classic general store would serve a community's basic merchandise needs; a companion business, such as Weeder & Compton, would repair cars, sell tires, and supply coal and coke (a coal-derived fuel that produced little or no smoke) for residents' stoves and furnaces. The culmination of this movement toward specialization is evident today, as the same site is now occupied by a restaurant that serves only pizza. (Historical image courtesy Clawson Historical Society.)

This 1920s view of Main Street (Livernois Avenue), looking south from Fourteen Mile Road, reveals evidence of a little remembered form of transit—the interurban. Operated by several different companies prior to the turn of the century, by 1900 ownership of all routes was consolidated by the Detroit United Railway. Filling a unique market niche, interurban trains were powered by overhead electrical lines and ran through Oakland County to points north, including Flint, Saginaw, and Port Huron—distances too near to be serviced by steam locomotive and too far for streetcar. Now just a memory, arteries such as Main Street reveal no trace of this feature from the history of transit. (Historical image courtesy Clawson Historical Society.)

Even the most astute viewer will find it difficult to realize that these two images are of the same location. In the 1923 view, looking west along Fourteen Mile Road, the intersection with Main Street (located between the small white structure and the drugstore) is barely discernable. The building on the left (with the overhead sign) serves as the link, as it is also visible in the contemporary image. The oldest extant building in downtown Clawson, the versatile structure has housed numerous types of businesses over the years, including a grocery store in 1923 and an architect's office today. (Historical image courtesy Clawson Historical Society.)

A major public-works effort in 1928 yielded more than just a widened Fourteen Mile Road. Since the project necessitated the removal of the commercial buildings on the street's north side, a strip of replacement storefronts was constructed first. With the ability to accommodate higher traffic volumes, the intersection of Fourteen Mile Road and Main Street became the community's focal point, capitalized by Sid's Drugs during the 1940s and the Black Lotus Bar today. (Historical image courtesy Clawson Historical Society.)

Public Act 164 of 1877 directed all Michigan cities and townships to establish and maintain public libraries and reading rooms for the benefit of the general public. Clawson was one of the first communities to implement this mandate. In the 1880s, the Blair family of Clawson bequeathed their family home for this purpose, which was appropriately named in their honor. The structure served the community until 1962, when it was replaced with a modern facility, which retained the original name. Thanks to the voters' recent approval of a library expansion bond, the building has recently doubled in size. (Historical image courtesy Clawson Historical Society.)

All across the Midwest are surviving examples of "kit homes" sold by major retailers during the early decades of the 20th century. From 1908 to 1940, Sears, Roebuck and Company was a major player in this industry, selling to new home owners a complete assortment of precut lumber, windows, masonry, and all other necessary components to construct a house. For a time, Sears even offered mortgage financing. The Vallonia model, a classic bungalow (pictured), originally sold for only \$2,100. This well-preserved Vallonia is a proud part of a Clawson neighborhood. (Ephemera courtesy Clawson Historical Society.)

Migration of Detroit's Jewish community into Oakland County began during the 1950s and continued for several decades. Congregation Shaarey Zedek built its architecturally stunning facility in Southfield in 1962 after having worshiped at six different sites in Detroit. The first image shows construction nearing completion. Visible in the modern view is the wooden Sukkah, a temporary structure used to observe Sukkoth, the Jewish celebration of the harvest. (Historical image courtesy the Archives of Congregation Shaarey Zedek.)

CHAPTER 2

NORTHWEST CORRIDOR

Despite its humble origins, the Southfield Police Department, shown here in the late-1950s, has evolved into one of the most professional law-enforcement agencies in Oakland County. Beginning in 1953 with just one officer and one patrol car (unequipped with a radio), the department soon moved into a renovated farmhouse that had no detention facilities. Prisoners were handcuffed to the drain of the water cooler until transferred. Today, the force has over 75 sworn officers and personnel who are, collectively, fluent in seven languages. (Historical image courtesy Southfield Public Library.)

When completed in 1954, Northland Center in Southfield represented a completely new shopping concept for area residents. A cluster of modern structures was envisioned, replete with amenities including courtyards with lush gardens and landscaping. Marshall Fredericks was one of six sculptors commissioned to design works of public art. His *Boy and Bear*, shaped in a manner inviting to children, has been an inspiration to generations of Northland patrons. The eventual enclosure of the mall took away none of the sculpture's charm. (Historical image courtesy Southfield Public Library.)

Northland was the first, and for many years the largest, major shopping mall in the nation. The center's western façade, facing Northwestern Highway, was once the stop for busses connecting Northland to the Detroit area's west side. Expansion of retail space on the main level during the 1970s forced the transit hub's relocation. Many customers, however, still use Macy's ground-level entrance. (Historical image courtesy Farmington Community Library.)

With a heritage going back over 50 years, Northland has witnessed several generations of shoppers, each sporting its unique customs. In the 1960s, shopping trips were often daylong, dressy affairs. In today's hectic world, shopping has become more of an errand and less an occasion, as the contrast in these images suggests. (Historical image courtesy Northland Center.)

By the late 1950s, suburban office architecture had matured to a high level of refinement. The 1959 Reynolds Metals Building showed the influence of a recent trip designer Minoru Yamasaki had taken to Asia and the Middle East, demonstrated in the beauty of the brise-soleil (permanent sunscreens) on the building's upper floors. The building's current use as a health club has necessitated little exterior alteration, testifying to the timelessness of the design. (Historical image courtesy Southfield Public Library.)

The lovingly restored Mary Thompson Farmhouse vividly brings to life the character of the 19th century. Mary Thompson, who was born in the house in 1871, led an accomplished life as an educator, eventually obtaining graduate degrees from Columbia University and New York University and teaching in various states. But she frequently returned to Southfield, where her family raised sheep and cattle on their farm. Living a disciplined life devoted to study and work, Mary never installed electricity or indoor plumbing. After her death in 1967, she willed the house and surrounding acreage to the City of Southfield. (Historical image courtesy Southfield Public Library.)

Much of Oakland County's heritage stems from the legacies of its houses of worship. Those still using the venerable old buildings generate special interest. One example is Southfield Presbyterian Church. The Southfield Associate Presbyterian Church was organized in 1850. Two years later, it purchased the building owned by Southfield Congregational Church and moved to its current location on Ten Mile Road, onto part of the farm owned by Ezekiel Hutton, an early member. Since a modern addition was built in 1963, the original church is now used as a chapel. Recently, the congregation merged with another Presbyterian church and is now known as Covenant Presbyterian. (Historical image courtesy Southfield Public Library.)

The Botsford Inn on Grand River Avenue, a structure harkening back to Michigan's pioneer days, stands proudly today, the beneficiary of a thoughtful restoration. Built in 1836 and purchased by Milton Botsford in 1852, the inn was a popular lodging place for early wayfarers traveling between Detroit and Lansing. In 1924, the landmark was acquired by Henry Ford, who had fond memories of the inn from his childhood. In 2007, after being acquired by nearby Botsford Hospital, the inn was restored to its 1924 appearance. Beautifully refurbished, the inn is now home to the Botsford Foundation, the hospital's fundraising arm. (Historical image courtesy Farmington Community Library.)

Lemuel and Lucy Botsford, Quaker farmers from Connecticut, moved to Michigan in 1836 and settled in the Farmington area. As the Botsford family rose to local prominence, their daughter Rhoda married P. Dean Warner, who was also from a family of community leaders. Their son, Fred M. Warner, would serve as governor of Michigan. (Historical image courtesy Farmington Community Library.)

Even before entering the Civic Theater in Farmington, the charm of the classic movie house is striking. Originally opened in 1940, it was designed by architect C. Howard Crane in the art moderne style. The Civic showed first-run movies until 1999, when it was purchased by the City of Farmington for various community functions. The city is very sensitive to the building's historical nature and carefully maintains its classic appearance. (Historical image courtesy Farmington Community Library.)

Nathan and Minerva Philbrick opened this beautiful Colonial-style tavern in 1827, and it quickly became a community focal point, often hosting local township meetings. Known for its high standard of food and service, the inn's second-floor ballroom attracted a steady flow of local patrons. Some anecdotal evidence suggests the Philbricks hosted escaped slaves during the era of the Underground Railroad, an act consistent with their Quaker faith. Today, the home closely resembles its 19th-century appearance and serves as a private residence. (Historical image courtesy Farmington Community Library.)

P. Dean Warner and Sarah Botsford Warner built this magnificent Victorian Italianate family home on Grand River Avenue in 1872. They would bequeath the home to their son Fred, who pursued a career in politics, serving in the Michigan Senate (1895–1898), as Michigan secretary of state (1901–1904), and three terms as governor (1905–1910). It was the era of progressive politics, and Warner advocated policies such as regulation of larger corporate interests, the outlawing of child labor, and women's suffrage. Today, the beautifully maintained home is owned by the City of Farmington and is used for weddings and other occasions. (Historical image courtesy Farmington Community Library.)

In 1830, officials of Farmington Township (which then included a full fifth of Oakland County) created five school districts and three "fractional" districts, each with a number roughly corresponding to the number of the township section in which it was located. The school built for Fractional District No. 1 was a single-room structure on Middlebelt Road. Remarkably, the building survives today and is used by nearby Hillel Day School. (Historical image courtesy Farmington Community Library.)

Planned and built in the early years of Oakland Community College (OCC), the elegant Orchard Ridge facility is the school's largest campus. Constructed in the California contemporary style, which is unusual for Michigan, the facility is the hub of OCC's system of five campuses, educating some 29,000 students per year—the largest community college enrollment in Michigan. Originally, the campus was illuminated by outdoor gas lamps, but they were soon replaced by electric lights to conserve energy. (Historical image courtesy Oakland Community College.)

In January 1967, the Universalist-Unitarian Church of Farmington was painstakingly moved from Warner Street near downtown Farmington to its new location off Halsted Road on the Gibson Centennial Farm. Organized in 1849, the church played a role in marshaling northern opposition to slavery. Several pro-suffrage meetings were held there, including one reportedly addressed by abolitionist Sojourner Truth. Still an active congregation, Farmington Universalist continues to advocate progressive social causes. (Historical image courtesy Farmington Community Library.)

In 1919, Detroit mayor James Couzens made a gift of $1.1 million to establish a new hospital and school for children in Farmington. Aimed primarily at serving patients with orthopedic afflictions, the institution earned a place as a center for excellence under the direction of Dr. William Blodgett. After the development of the Salk vaccine for polio in the mid-1950s, the need for the hospital diminished. Today, the Albert Kahn–designed structure is the centerpiece of the Botsford Continuing Health Center, a place devoted to serving seniors with varying degrees of independence. (Historical image courtesy Farmington Community Library.)

In 1923, Detroit realtor Louise Lathrup Kelley purchased approximately 1,000 acres in what was then Southfield Township to create the Lathrup Townsite (incorporated today as the City of Lathrup Village), an upscale planned community with strict regulations concerning home construction, street and lot dimensions, and the like. Shortly after this, she published a book titled *The Gateway to Happiness* extolling the virtues of her project. A focal point of the community was the Lathrup Homestead, where Kelley and her family resided and which for a time served as the municipal offices. In 2008, the structure was gutted by fire. (Historical image courtesy Lathrup Village Historical Society.)

Southfield Road, running through the center of the Lathrup Townsite, was the location of the town hall, which served as the community's sales office. Unfortunately, Kelley's stringent rules included restrictive deed covenants that excluded virtually all religious and racial minorities. Unenforceable today, these and all other attributes of the Lathrup community provide insight into the phenomena of pre–World War II suburbanization. Recently, the hall was demolished to make way for a strip shopping center. (Historical and contemporary images courtesy Lathrup Village Historical Society.)

A longtime fixture on the shores of Sylvan Lake, the Oakland County Boat Club (OCBC) is a little-known treasure. Founded in 1912, with the clubhouse dating to 1917, the OCBC has hosted generations of boating enthusiasts. During World War II, gas rationing forced a shift from powerboats to sailboats, while today the club hosts a combination of each. In 1919, the clubhouse was rotated 90 degrees. At one time standing on pilings with boat wells underneath, the structure was moved back 70 feet in 1932. These moves account for the different angles of the two images. (Historical image courtesy Oakland County Boat Club.)

In 1877, Gen. Joseph Tarr Copeland sold his home near Orchard Lake (which had served as a hotel for a time) to Gen. J. Sumner Rodgers, a military professor, to establish the Michigan Military Academy, which he patterned after West Point. In 1879, commencement speaker Gen. William Tecumseh Sherman of Civil War fame coined the famous phrase "War is Hell" during his speech. Today, Copeland's castle-like home and several surrounding buildings serve as a Catholic seminary. (Historical image courtesy Orchard Lake Schools.)

In 1900, several buildings were added to the campus, including one that served as the post office, which is shown here in the 1920s. After bankruptcy forced the academy to close in 1908, the campus became the home of SS. Cyril and Methodius Seminary, a Catholic institution educating a primarily Polish student body. Today, the old post office serves as the school's administration building. (Historical image courtesy Orchard Lake Schools.)

Elders at Kirk in the Hills in Bloomfield Township beam with pride as a portion of their new carillon waits to be hoisted atop the tower in 1960. The 77-bell behemoth, cast in the Netherlands, was a donation by members Roy and Ruth Fruehauf, a prominent family in the Detroit area's automotive history. After a tedious three-month installation, a dedication concert was held, which began the tradition of summer carillon concerts performed annually by guest artists. (Historical image courtesy Kirk in the Hills.)

CHAPTER 3

Points North

Bloomfield Hills is internationally noted for its stunning residential architecture. One example is the Gordon Saunders house, designed by legendary architect Alden Dow. Dow, a protégé of Frank Lloyd Wright, produced designs similar to his mentor, but with an increased use of unusual angles, intending to create a visually interesting appearance. The Saunders home was in fact nicknamed the "House of a Thousand Angles" and was featured in *Life* magazine in March of 1948. (Courtesy Walter Reuther Library, Wayne State University.)

Few mysteries are as enduring in southeast Michigan as the disappearance of Teamsters president Jimmy Hoffa on July 30, 1975. Hoffa's prison sentence for jury tampering was commuted by Pres. Richard Nixon in 1971, under the condition he abstain from involvement in union affairs until 1980. Shortly thereafter, however, he began exploring possible ways of circumventing this obstacle. On the fateful day, Hoffa left for what he said was a lunch meeting at the Machus Red Fox with rivals Anthony Giacalone and Anthony Provenzano. Hoffa was never seen again, and his two companions denied such a meeting was ever planned. The ensuing investigation lasted for years, involving federal, state, and local authorities. Shortly after his disappearance, the FBI used the restaurant's banquet rooms as temporary offices. (Historical image courtesy Scott Burnstein.)

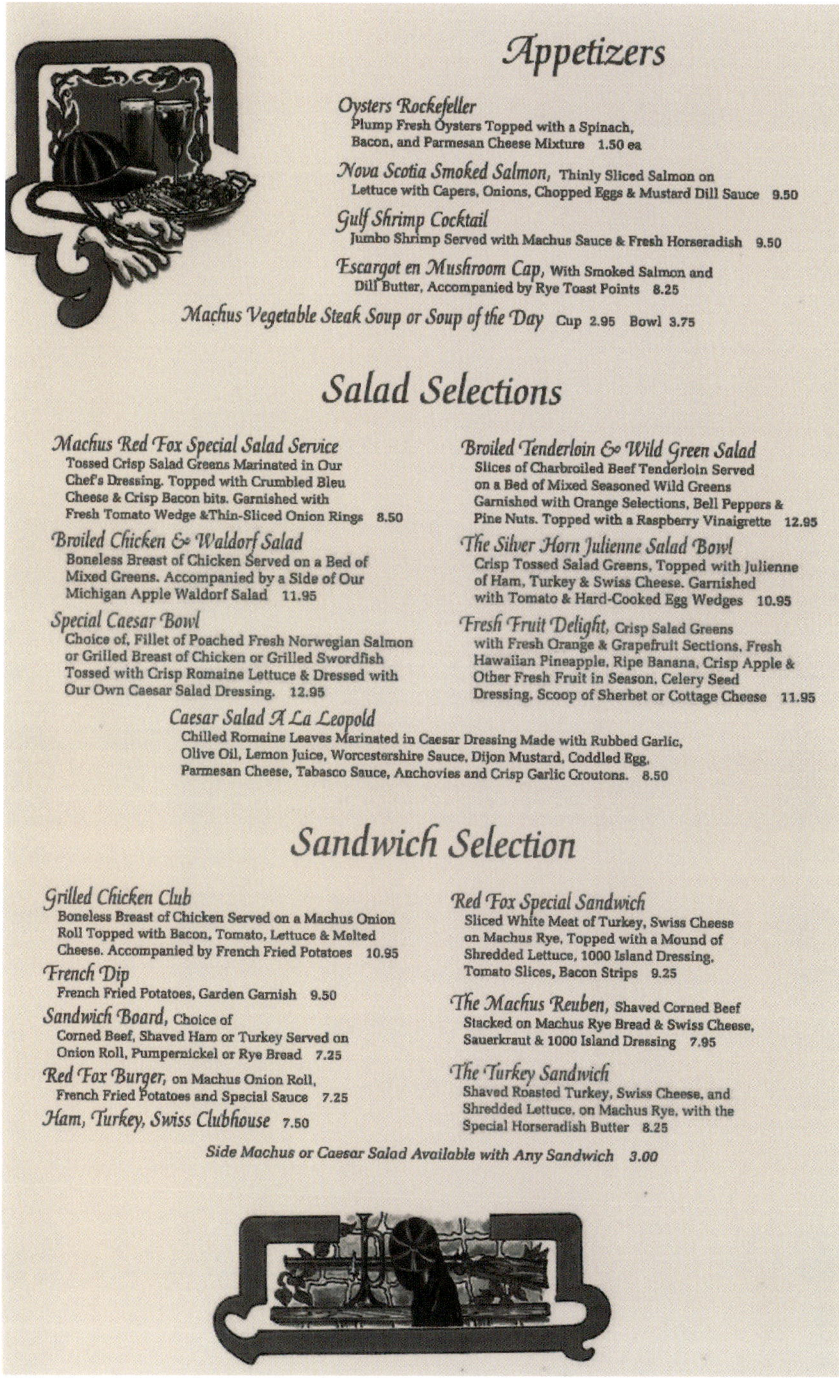

Appetizers

Oysters Rockefeller
Plump Fresh Oysters Topped with a Spinach, Bacon, and Parmesan Cheese Mixture 1.50 ea

Nova Scotia Smoked Salmon, Thinly Sliced Salmon on Lettuce with Capers, Onions, Chopped Eggs & Mustard Dill Sauce 9.50

Gulf Shrimp Cocktail
Jumbo Shrimp Served with Machus Sauce & Fresh Horseradish 9.50

Escargot en Mushroom Cap, With Smoked Salmon and Dill Butter, Accompanied by Rye Toast Points 8.25

Machus Vegetable Steak Soup or Soup of the Day Cup 2.95 Bowl 3.75

Salad Selections

Machus Red Fox Special Salad Service
Tossed Crisp Salad Greens Marinated in Our Chef's Dressing. Topped with Crumbled Bleu Cheese & Crisp Bacon bits. Garnished with Fresh Tomato Wedge &Thin-Sliced Onion Rings 8.50

Broiled Chicken & Waldorf Salad
Boneless Breast of Chicken Served on a Bed of Mixed Greens. Accompanied by a Side of Our Michigan Apple Waldorf Salad 11.95

Special Caesar Bowl
Choice of, Fillet of Poached Fresh Norwegian Salmon or Grilled Breast of Chicken or Grilled Swordfish Tossed with Crisp Romaine Lettuce & Dressed with Our Own Caesar Salad Dressing. 12.95

Broiled Tenderloin & Wild Green Salad
Slices of Charbroiled Beef Tenderloin Served on a Bed of Mixed Seasoned Wild Greens Garnished with Orange Selections, Bell Peppers & Pine Nuts. Topped with a Raspberry Vinaigrette 12.95

The Silver Horn Julienne Salad Bowl
Crisp Tossed Salad Greens, Topped with Julienne of Ham, Turkey & Swiss Cheese. Garnished with Tomato & Hard-Cooked Egg Wedges 10.95

Fresh Fruit Delight, Crisp Salad Greens with Fresh Orange & Grapefruit Sections, Fresh Hawaiian Pineapple, Ripe Banana, Crisp Apple & Other Fresh Fruit in Season. Celery Seed Dressing. Scoop of Sherbet or Cottage Cheese 11.95

Caesar Salad A La Leopold
Chilled Romaine Leaves Marinated in Caesar Dressing Made with Rubbed Garlic, Olive Oil, Lemon Juice, Worcestershire Sauce, Dijon Mustard, Coddled Egg, Parmesan Cheese, Tabasco Sauce, Anchovies and Crisp Garlic Croutons. 8.50

Sandwich Selection

Grilled Chicken Club
Boneless Breast of Chicken Served on a Machus Onion Roll Topped with Bacon, Tomato, Lettuce & Melted Cheese. Accompanied by French Fried Potatoes 10.95

French Dip
French Fried Potatoes, Garden Garnish 9.50

Sandwich Board, Choice of Corned Beef, Shaved Ham or Turkey Served on Onion Roll, Pumpernickel or Rye Bread 7.25

Red Fox Burger, on Machus Onion Roll, French Fried Potatoes and Special Sauce 7.25

Ham, Turkey, Swiss Clubhouse 7.50

Red Fox Special Sandwich
Sliced White Meat of Turkey, Swiss Cheese on Machus Rye, Topped with a Mound of Shredded Lettuce, 1000 Island Dressing, Tomato Slices, Bacon Strips 9.25

The Machus Reuben, Shaved Corned Beef Stacked on Machus Rye Bread & Swiss Cheese, Sauerkraut & 1000 Island Dressing 7.95

The Turkey Sandwich
Shaved Roasted Turkey, Swiss Cheese, and Shredded Lettuce, on Machus Rye, with the Special Horseradish Butter 8.25

Side Machus or Caesar Salad Available with Any Sandwich 3.00

The Machus Red Fox closed in 1996, reflecting a shift in consumer tastes. Today, the location is home to Andiamo, one of a number of local Italian bistros. During its heyday, however, the Red Fox reined as one of the preeminent spots in Oakland County for traditional expense-account meals, offering truly classic American fare to support the closing of innumerable business deals, as reflected by this period menu. The menu dates from 1992, but the items are much the same as in 1975. (Courtesy Robert Machus.)

Long recognized as one of the preeminent Jewish congregations in Michigan, Temple Beth El traces its roots to 1850, when it was formed in Detroit as the Beth El Society. Over time, the synagogue moved several times, along with the congregation. This trend continued until 1973, when Temple Beth El left Detroit for its magnificent new location in Bloomfield Township. Designed by legendary architect Minoru Yamasaki, the structure represents the tent used to house the Ark of the Covenant by the ancient Israelites. (Historical image courtesy Rabbi Leo M. Franklin Archives, Temple Beth El.)

In 1904, Ellen Scripps Booth (daughter of *Detroit News* founder James Scripps) and her husband, George Booth, began Cranbrook, a planned community of artists and educational institutions in Bloomfield Hills that was patterned after a school in England by the same name. In 1925, Booth persuaded Finnish architect Eliel Saarinen (1873–1950) to design most of the campus's buildings, which represent a blend of the classic Tudor and Arts and Crafts styles. In 1928, Saarinen also designed his own personal residence, a testimony of the architect's depth of innovation; the home was built between 1929 and 1930. In the years after Saarinen's death, modifications inconsistent with his intentions can be seen in the vintage (1978) image. Recently, the home has been restored to the artist's original vision. (Historical image courtesy Walter Reuther Library, Wayne State University; contemporary image, Cranbrook Art Museum/Balthazar Korab.)

In 1931, Saarinen recruited sculptor Carl Milles to join the faculty as sculptor in residence. He remained until 1952, simultaneously teaching, crafting pieces for the campus, and accepting commissions from clients worldwide. Eventually, Milles created some 70 pieces for the grounds, virtually of all of which remain today. Perhaps his most recognizable, the *Orpheus* fountain, flanks the propylaeum between the art academy's museum and library. A campus focal point for decades, the sculpture's neighboring buildings are now undergoing an extensive renovation. (Historical image courtesy Walter Reuther Library, Wayne State University.)

Booth's vision included facilities to support all facets of a quality education, including athletics. In this 1930s image, the school's field house and related facilities are near completion. Even here, Cranbrook's artistic emphasis is apparent, exemplified by two sculptures of a Greek discus thrower flanking the track. The school has studiously maintained this tradition by expertly preserving the facilities and adding new ones, including the stunning natatorium that was completed in 1999. (Historical image courtesy Walter Reuther Library, Wayne State University.)

Perhaps the most unusual feature at Cranbrook is the outdoor Greek theater, one of very few in the United States. Designed by Marcus Burrows and opened in 1915, the full-size reproduction of an ancient theater is believed to have been inspired by ruins found in Mt. Taormina, Sicily. For decades, the venue has been used for both classical and contemporary productions by various Cranbrook entities. In 1932, Henry Scripps Booth founded St. Dunstan's Theatre Guild, which presents outdoor shows during the warm-weather months. Like much of Cranbrook, the theater has recently undergone a thoughtful restoration. (Historical image courtesy Walter Reuther Library, Wayne State University; modern image, St. Dunstan's Theatre.)

The Birmingham Theater has had several incarnations that reflect the changing nature of its host community. Originally opened in 1927 as a traditional movie house, the venue transitioned to live entertainment in 1972 and finally to an eight-screen multiplex in 1996. Along with its sister facility, the Palladium 8, which is two blocks away, the Birmingham's changes have reflected the community's emergence as an entertainment destination. (Historical image courtesy Walter Reuther Library, Wayne State University.)

By the mid-1950s, downtown Birmingham had become an upscale shopping destination, anchored by exclusive stores such as Jacobson's. In later years, these stores would grow in number and Jacobson's would add a second floor. The 1990s, however, saw increased competition from shopping areas such as the Somerset Collection, prompting Birmingham to reinvent itself. Jacobson's fell victim to this trend, forcing it into bankruptcy in 2005. The building today has been creatively reused by McCann Worldwide Advertising. (Historical image courtesy Walter Reuther Library, Wayne State University.)

The exclusive nature of Birmingham shopping can be seen in this 1965 image. The Village Shop, a woman's boutique, is next door to Hack Shoes, a children's shoe store specializing in serving difficult-to-fit youngsters. Today, in a less staid but still upscale atmosphere, the street plays host to art galleries, restaurants, and the Scandia Home shop. Yuletide shoppers especially enjoy the ambiance of Pierce Street. (Historical image courtesy Walter Reuther Library, Wayne State University.)

During the early 20th century, the railroad corridor between Detroit and Pontiac grew in importance as both passenger and freight traffic expanded. In the early 1920s, the main line was moved east from Woodward to its current location. In 1931, this charming Tudor Revival train station opened to serve passengers. After functioning for several decades, the facility closed in 1978 as other modes of transportation became dominant. The building reopened in 1984 as an upscale restaurant and is now known as the Big Rock Chophouse. The lush landscaping is a recent addition. (Historical image courtesy Walter Reuther Library, Wayne State University.)

In the early 1920s, prominent women in Birmingham saw the need for a facility large enough to accommodate art exhibits, plays, weddings, meetings, and other occasions. After renting a small house two blocks away, the group opened the current Community House to the public in 1930. Over the decades, the house has played host to many affairs, including lectures, business functions, and high school proms. In 1990, a historically sympathetic addition was added to the building's north side, doubling its size. (Historical image courtesy Walter Reuther Library, Wayne State University.)

Dating to its founding as a gristmill in 1837, the Franklin Cider Mill has captivated Oakland County residents for generations. Constructed and operated by Col. Peter Van Every, the mill served local farmers throughout most of the 19th century as the only facility in the area for grinding wheat. Purchased by James Flynn in 1914, the mill switched to pressing apples for cider, using a water-powered press driven by a nearby branch of the Rouge River. The mill has changed hands several times since and has undergone some modernization, but it retains its nostalgic charm, evidenced every fall season with different events, including a symphony concert. (Historical image courtesy Franklin Historical Society.)

While other small communities in metro Detroit retain a quaint, small-town atmosphere, none matches Franklin's frozen-in-time character. Founded in 1825, the intimate community features small, independent shops, a volunteer fire department, and homes dating from the 19th century. These two images, taken some 40 years apart, illustrate Franklin's apparent immunity to change. (Historical image courtesy Franklin Historical Society.)

School Hill, the location of the old Franklin School on Franklin Road, has its own unique history. The original school building was erected in 1845 to serve area children and was replaced by a larger facility in 1869. When that structure burned in 1922, the current school was built, which eventually absorbed into the Birmingham Public School District. After closing in 1979 due to declining enrollment, the building was purchased by the Muslim community and today functions as the Huda School and Montessori, an Islamic parochial school. (Historical image courtesy Franklin Historical Society.)

As the Birmingham-Troy area grew in affluence during the 1960s and 1970s, upscale shopping venues were established to tap this economic opportunity. In 1967, Saks Fifth Avenue opened a store at Coolidge Highway and Big Beaver Road in Troy. Two years later, Saks was joined by Bonwitt Teller, which were then connected by Somerset Mall. In 1992, Neiman Marcus replaced Bonwitt's and a second floor was added to the mall. In 1996, a three-level companion mall was built across Big Beaver Road, featuring dozens of new stores including Michigan's first Nordstrom. The new facility is connected to the original mall by an efficient moving skywalk. (Historical image courtesy Somerset Collection.)

As the early signs of Oakland County's growth became apparent, so did the need for new cemeteries. In 1928, Clarence Sanger dedicated White Chapel Cemetery in Troy. Established as the nation's first memorial park east of California (where the concept was developed), White Chapel was intended as a place that celebrates life rather than grieving over death. All grave markers are flush with the ground, which allows memorials to various military and fraternal groups to be visible. Elegant white marble chapels and fountains add to the aesthetically pleasing environment. Notable figures interred at White Chapel include architect Albert Kahn, industrialist John DeLorean, and radio personality J.P. McCarthy. (Historical Image courtesy Pontiac Public Library.)

As many auto-related businesses were migrating to the Oakland suburbs during the 1950s and 1960s, auto dealer Frank Audette sought to capitalize on the trend. In 1960, he purchased a large tract of land along Maple Road, opened his Pontiac dealership, and gradually sold parcels to other retailers, representing different nameplates to create the Troy Motor Mall, one of the largest groupings of car dealers anywhere; it continues to thrive. Audette was the son-in-law of Edward Fisher, one of the famous Fisher brothers who established Fisher Body Company in the early 1900s. (Historical image courtesy Somerset Buick GMC.)

The Fox & Hounds Restaurant, a longtime symbol of affluence in Bloomfield Hills, closed in 2007 after an impressive 80-year run. Upon its opening in 1927, the building housed shops, apartments, and hotel rooms, as well as a restaurant. The second-floor banquet rooms saw dozens of weddings, showers, and other celebrations. At present, the site is being redeveloped into a mixed-use office and retail building that, in a nod to the site's past, sports the rich Bavarian-style architectural featured in the original structure. (Historical image courtesy Walter Reuther Library, Wayne State University.)

CHAPTER 4

FARTHER AFIELD

As the aviation era unfolded, Oakland County established itself as an early leader in 1928 with the founding of what was then Pontiac Municipal Airport. Evolving into a "reliever" facility for the purpose of serving individuals and businesses, the airport grew along with the greater community. In 1967, it was acquired by Oakland County and renamed Oakland County International Airport. With over 144,000 annual takeoffs and landings, it now ranks as the second-busiest airport in Michigan. (Historical image courtesy Oakland Pioneer Historical Society.)

In 1854, the first Baptist congregation in Rochester was organized in Stoney Creek (near present-day Utica). Around 1870, members purchased an unfinished church, moved it to its current site at Walnut Boulevard and Fourth Street, and completed the construction. The congregation worshipped at this site in Rochester for over a century, moving to a modern structure on Orion Road in 1973. In a creative reuse, the former church is now home to the Village Shoe Inn, a women's shoe store. (Historical Image courtesy Rochester Hills Community Library.)

One of the oldest structures in Rochester, the "Opera House," as it has been traditionally known, opened in November 1890 and served as the cultural hub of the small community. The auditorium on the second floor offered movies, lectures, dances, and the like, but no opera was ever performed there. The storefronts at street level housed various businesses over the years, including the pharmacy and bank in the vintage image. Restored in 1987, the building is home to Lytle Pharmacy, and a law office occupies the second floor. (Historical Image courtesy Rochester Hills Community Library.)

In an image from the 1920s, a car rumbles down Rochester Road (Main Street) over the Clinton River. In the pre-automotive era, the Clinton, along with Stoney and Paint Creeks, provided for Rochester's economic growth by powering several lumber, grist, and cider mills. Several plank roads linking Rochester to the communities of Detroit, Pontiac, and Royal Oak allowed easy access for farmers and other tradesmen. Today, the charm of Rochester's history surrounds Main Street and provides the town with much of its character. (Historical Image courtesy Rochester Hills Community Library.)

Purchased by auto magnate John Dodge and his wife, Matilda, in 1908, along with 320 surrounding acres, this home served as their weekend residence for several years. It eventually became the clubhouse of the adjacent nine-hole golf course that John built. The course fell into disrepair following Dodge's death but was restored in the 1970s and integrated with a new 18-hole facility. Today, the home serves as Oakland University's office of alumni affairs. (Historical Image courtesy Rochester Hills Community Library.)

After John Dodge's death, Matilda married her second husband, Alfred Wilson, in 1925. They lived in the old clubhouse while their nearby home, the palatial Meadowbrook Hall, was being built. Matilda commissioned architect William Kapp of Smith, Hinchman & Gryllis of Detroit to design the 110-room Tudor Revival mansion, and she personally supervised its construction. In 1957, the Wilsons bequeathed Meadowbrook to Michigan State University with the proviso that they be allowed to live there until their deaths. It now serves as a popular venue for weddings, conferences, and other university functions. (Historical image courtesy Oakland University archives.)

The Wilson's 1957 bequest also included over 1,500 surrounding acres, various farm buildings, and $2 million to establish a satellite campus of Michigan State University. After its formative years, the school achieved its own identity as Oakland University when it graduated its first class in 1963. Today, Oakland offers baccalaureate degrees in over 120 fields of study, as well as another 100 professional and graduate programs. In 2011, the university will open a medical school in conjunction with William Beaumont Hospital. (Historical image courtesy Oakland University archives.)

The image from Oakland University's early years displays a formal procession of faculty across the still mostly empty campus. Over the years, generous support from alumni, benefactors, and the State of Michigan have made expansion of the school possible, including the recent addition to the Kresge Library (background). At the first commencement in 1963, founder Matilda Dodge Wilson presented each graduate with a diamond ring. (Historical image courtesy Oakland University archives.)

As the Depression's grip weakened by the late 1930s, downtown Pontiac's shopping district showed signs of revival. In 1938, Chase's Department Store opened its elegant Art Deco building at 54 East Saginaw Street to great acclaim, offering an upscale alternative to nearby Kresge and Woolworth. During the next few years, Chase's became a community institution, which unfortunately came to an unceremonious end on September 21, 1942, when a fire of unknown origin gutted the popular store. Today, the block is the site of support facilities for Pontiac Osteopathic Hospital. (Historical Image courtesy Pontiac Public Library.)

Like many American cities, Pontiac's downtown has lost some of its vitality in recent decades. These two contrasting, west-facing views of Huron Street show a more compact urban core in the vintage image, while open space is visible in the modern photograph, allowing the offices of the *Oakland Press* to be seen on the left. However, two major landmarks that still proudly standing are the Riker Building on the right and the First Presbyterian Church on the left, both occupied today. (Historical Image courtesy Pontiac Public Library.)

Even in a working-class city like Pontiac, the formality of the 1920s is evident in this vintage image of the corner of Saginaw and Lawrence Streets. The suited gentleman standing on the sidewalk, combined with the cigar shop, conveys a feeling of sophistication common to the era but increasingly rare today. The present-day Coney Island restaurant on the corner illustrates the grab-and-go culture now favored by downtown workers. (Historical image courtesy Pontiac Public Library.)

By the early 1960s, community leaders in Oakland County determined that the population shift from Detroit and the postwar emphasis on higher education would necessitate the establishment of a community college. After being approved by voters in 1964, the new Oakland Community College established its first two campuses from preexisting facilities. The Highland Lakes campus in Waterford was crafted from the abandoned Oakland County Tuberculosis Sanitarium. Highland Hall, as the main building came to be known, now serves a variety of functions, including housing the campus police station. (Historical image courtesy Oakland Community College.)

What had been the sanitarium's nurses' residence was included in the renovation. Together with Highland Hall, High Oaks Hall was modified to house the college's library, bookstore, offices, and classrooms. The college's first allied health programs were also offered here, providing an interesting link to the site's past. Today, Highland and High Oaks Halls blend beautifully with more modern buildings, creating an efficient yet aesthetically pleasing campus. (Historical image courtesy Oakland Community College.)

An even more radical transition was required at the Auburn Hills campus, which had been a former Nike missile base. Abandoned by the military due to its obsolescence, the buildings were renovated to house various technical programs, such as computer science and manufacturing technology. Today, the former barracks are gone, and the site is now home to OCC's Combined Regional Emergency Services Training (CREST) facility. A state-of-the-art training center for police and emergency first responders, CREST is a mock town complete with furnished homes, a convenience store, and a fire-training tower. It even includes a faux Bank of America branch (identified as office No. 007) where bank-robbery drills are held. (Historical image courtesy Oakland Community College.)

BIBLIOGRAPHY

Begney, John. *Dreams and Visions–Kirk in the Hills, the First Fifty Years*. Bloomfield Hills, MI: Clark Graphics, 1997.

"Chase's Hit by Early Morning Blaze." *Pontiac Daily Press*. November 16, 1942.

Gallagher, John and Eric J. Hill. *AIA Guide: the American Institute of Architects Guide to Detroit Architecture*. Detroit: Wayne State University Press, 2003.

Gavrilovich, Peter and Bill McGraw, eds. *The Detroit Almanac: 300 Years of Life in the Motor City*. Detroit: Detroit Free Press, 2000.

Hagman, Arthur, ed. *Oakland County Book of History*. Pontiac, MI: Oakland County Board of Commission, 1970.

Hutting, Rev. A.M. *Shrine of the Little Flower Souvenir Book*. Royal Oak, MI: Radio League of the Little Flower, 1936.

schools.cranbrook.edu/podium

The Story of Beaumont: The Next Chapter. Royal Oak, MI: William Beaumont Hospital, 2000.

A Vision of Excellence: Oakland Community College. Midland, MI: The McKay Press, 2000.

www.bigrockchophouse.com

www.botsford.org

www.ci.birmingham.mi.us

www.oakland.edu

www.oaklandcountyboatclub.roundtablelive.org

www.searsarchives.com/homes/index.htm

www.uufarmington.org

www.whitechapelcemetery.com/legacy.htm